Night Talks

Sharmila McNulty-Sharma

BookLeaf
Publishing

India | USA | UK

Night Talks © 2022

Sharmila McNulty-Sharma

Presentation by *BookLeaf Publishing*

Web: www.bookleafpub.com

E-mail: info@bookleafpub.com

ISBN : 9789358360868

First edition 2022

*For the unquiet minds that rouse
at night,*

Not knowing what to say or write,

*Perhaps these words will give a
voice*

To our kindred thoughts.

Acknowledgement

My mother, for encouraging creative expression from childhood.

Liam, for your consideration and love when listening to every poem I've ever written.

Elias, my present and future inspiration.

My greatest friend Ashna Bajaj, for being a cheerleader come rain, or shine.

Sylvia Plath and Rupi Kaur, for keeping my love of poetry alive, and for creating a platform for future female poets.

And, Mr J M McDonald, for reminding me that my love for poetry is to be celebrated; not ignored.

Preface

This collection of poetry was written after the birth of my first son, and offers a raw and unrestrained insight into my post-partum state of mind: from resentment to gratitude. Whist compiling this collection, I found most of my ideas surfaced late at night, or in the early morning hours, when the quiet permitted my mind space to breathe.

Being a first-time mother during a pandemic brought new value to my relationships and my appreciation of the natural world, leading me to want to express these feelings in written form. I truly enjoyed writing this cathartic collection, as it was a reminder that I will never be alone in my feelings as a mother, partner and fellow woman.

I hope that the poems in this collection find their own way of connecting to you, whether it's our quiet feelings, strongest beliefs, or our unique expressions of love which bring us together.

Billions of atoms entered the earth when
you were born.

Like a firework:
A sudden, violent crack
In a bed of red roses.

The world never shrunk back.
No plan was ever executed finely
And this was only ever decided:
Divine timing.

Strontium, lithium,
A raging kilonova
Joining us together
Prayers ringing in our ears.

You are the final glowing embers on a

cold night,

The one that crowds rush to see

Your soft fingers clinging onto me

Fingernails digging in apprehensively.

Bolting blue eyes staring through the

dark space.

So, I paint pictures of your face.

And hold you near,

So that the sparks won't disappear.

2am

Stolen time.

To stay awake

And sit in stillness.

Where only your steady breath

Echoes around the room.

This is my sanctuary.

Here, I am me.

No one's mother, sister, daughter, lover.

Nothing but warm blood,

I am free.

Forever yours

This bump
Where you were
Is supposed to make me feel unworthy.

A reminder that I haven't yet
'Bounced back' after carrying you for
nine-long - months.

Cardio is meant to help
Perhaps, a diet too
Yet, when I look in the mirror
I'm reminded of you
And every tiny kick, hiccup and
heartbeat
So, to me, it will do.

I will take the frumpy pictures
And accept a new dress size
I'll ignore the stares at my misshapen
figure.
Even from my own critical eye.

For your home,
Your beautiful home,
Will always be honoured by
This soft and warm bump
Where you once were
Where you may rest your head

Whenever you need to return,

Forever yours.

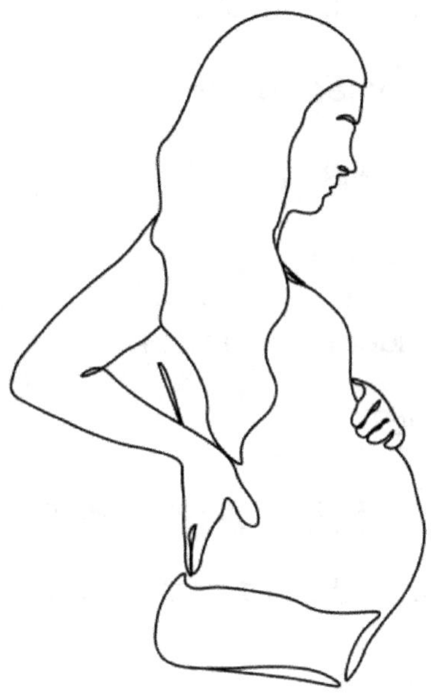

Your eyes

Blue, the first time we saw you

Fading into a misty grey

Large and unapologetic

Wide and aware.

What wonder is in that stare?

What logic?

A greening sea of self-discovery

Being stitched to your father's identity.

'He will look like his daddy',

They say.

'He looks like you now',

They muse.

'I hope he has light eyes',

They pray.

I dig my fingers into the earth

You copy -

Smothering us both in brown

My ancestors wear this crown

The colour of the earth in their eyes

The sky looks down to see it

The branches of the Banyan tree reach
towards it

This colour is my home:

The motherland.

Yes, my eyes are brown,

Like the colour of melted sugar

Like sweet cocoa

Like cinnamon sticks

Like the humble acorn

Like crisp autumn leaves.

And if it should be

That your eyes voyage

From the ocean to the land

Like life did all that time ago

I shall still take your face in my palm

And tell you,

I love your eyes.

Grandpa

When the body fails,

And loved ones are left behind

After two generations,

What memories survive?

What understanding,

What love prevails?

Only that which are told

Through reminiscent tales.

A picture on a wall,

A visited grave,

A bench in the park,

A teacup saved.

But, to honour you,

We gave him your name:

Peter.

Naniji's house

My child's toys are scattered around the
floor

Bowls of food placed to

explore

Contained tenderness.

Inside these walls

Where I grew up

The smell of tadka in my hair

Haldi stains on my nails

Danya waiting to be picked

The kitchen still spills out plenty

Cupboards never empty.

O, she keeps on giving.

Soft arms wrapped around him

Swinging in the evening sun

Sunlight on her greying hair.

I remember when I sat there

On her loving lap

Facing God

And now, in my mother's home

I stand and watch

My mother being reborn,

As my child sits upon her throne

A world of love at his fingertips.

Tease me

Tease me for the smell of onion in my
hair

The garlic under my fingernails

The green stains of dhania on my skin.

Tell me I stink

Of cauliflower, curry or cloves

Throw your abuse in droves

At the spices on my clothes

Then walk into my mother's home

Where the warm candles glow,

and incense burns

And the tadka dhal churns on the stove

Tell me then, when her food melts on
your tongue and your belly is full

Why I should feel ashamed

Of the scents of home.

Night talks

It is time for the truth.

That word which pricks you with fear;

crumbles walls; summons tsunamis.

Yes.

It is best served fresh.

In-the-moment truth,

Not tomorrow-truth,

You and I, right here.

Now.

Lend me your ears,

I'll give you my right side and speak

On each live switch clicking at the
forefront of my mind.

Shall we begin with your distortion of time?

Or deceptive tendencies?

A lack of veracity?

Perhaps, I can unpick each thread of this tapestry, to show you your own mythological story, in technicolour.

Your sighs of frustration at what must only be called Duty.

Why is it so hard now for us to heed the call?

To meet the criteria of what, or who we need to be?

To listen to the words of a woman,

Who only wants what's best for you

Who only wants what's best

Who only wants,

Not needs,

or demands anything from you?

Tonight, truth be told; you know it's true.

But, who only ever told the gospel
truth?

Receipts

I store them

To consider, when it possesses my mind.

Memorabilia of self-torture,

Or a caution, to not ignore.

Don't get

Too comfortable.

Am I the only one

Who chooses to resurrect misery?

To wallow in the disquieting past?

It's as if by forgetting I'd become…

More vulnerable and less numb

To what you may, or may not do next.

To what you have done so
thoughtlessly.

They are the ignition of my flaws:

The quiet questions

The incarceration

The sickness.

They speak.

Yet, it is your voice mocking me.

I look for more, and you feel it.

You're afraid of what bones I'll uncover.

So, you return, backspace,

As if that will rewrite the past.

A swift cover over the evidence.
Because you need this exchange of
energy to last.

Can the mind not

Undo

Undo

Undo?

Let me be ignorant too.

It was you

Who played the wrong move,

I simply took my turn.

Oh, what a fool I am to see truth in your
musings.

Still, I give some credence to your
claims,

Perhaps that's my mother's blood in
me.

You see,

Judas' name went down in history,

The betrayal of an innocent loved one
can tarnish you forever

And yet, we are asked to forgive.

More fool the life that we live.

If they were paper I would burn them all

And likely regret it

So, I store each receipt as a memory of
what you do.

As a way to return to the flawed you

Should I ever choose

To let go.

925

The words I speak are silver

Disguised in a thin layer of gold.

Solid and untold, a secret pool of
unicorn blood.

Can you taste their worth?

On a summer's evening, when slices of
sunlight streak the sky

Like a softened humbug, no longer
willing to take the bitterness away,

They stick,

these words,

to the inside of my fingers, to the nape
of my neck,

and around my ankle. And when the air
gets to them, I will oxidise too.

Turning blue to brown for you.

Yet, you will never listen, to the value of
my tongue.

So, I paint my silver words with gold,

And sell them

to the highest bidder.

Circe

True love never dies
Oh, but it does
I felt it go
Like a crack in the hull,
Or a volcano turning cold
All faculties paused.

The realisation: a thread
Slipping out of the eye of a needle,
The moirai watching
One well-timed snip.

Was it a blip? No.
And, I did know it was true.
For so long I thought there was no one
else but you.

Every love lyric, every rhyme
All-consuming, blinding love,
Which has now unwound;
Is left sprawled on the floor

Destiny keeps knocking at my door.
What a waste to wait in stagnant water.
But I'll stand for a minute for you all,
 To see, as you'll likely not listen to me.

Look at the leeches clutching to my feet.
Hear the vultures calling carrion above.
They smell the stench of this rotten love.

Still, you'll not admit defeat.

For most, it is too easy to repeat the lie,

that true love never dies

Glass jar

Who painted that uniform on you?

The intimidating yellow and black,

Much like your cousin, but not an exact
match.

Was it God?

Did he know that in order for you to
succeed you must be feared?

Still, you have the upper hand,

To fight without the fear of death.

An evolutionary genius!

Isn't that a stab at Zeus?

Perhaps, Melissa would be pleased.

Though, we all know, you are not worthy
of love like the bees. For their flowing
honey and their coevality with the trees.

3am

On the green sofa

Under the wool throw

I consider how to get through

To you

The night is cool

The breeze flows

Between the pane and panel

Of our broken window

A spider's web twitches.

A light bulb glitches.

I'm not ready yet.

Please, go back to bed.

Boomerang

You throw words at me

And then take them back

Fingers twisting the inside of the
cassette

Rewinding the blackened tape.

And here I am with my pen

Adding to your glossary of insults

Embossed and in bold type.

It's going to be a long night.

How could I escape?

I ask.

Did I tempt fate?

Perhaps.

You don't care what's at stake.

But when my pages are full,

And the ink is dry

Maybe then you'll want to see

Your words: glitching phonemes to me,

My screaming desire to cry

The last word

Goodbye.

Sitting still

Yes, I'm in my favourite asana

But can we talk about you?

The position you have knotted and
pulled yourself into

Has dragged me with it

And, somehow, I've survived.

But, a small piece of me has been
stained purple

Like a bruise, or perhaps like silk.

Either way, I'm here, and you're around:

Tasting thin and looking like the trunk of
a tree,

You're only good food when someone
else is feeding me.

Tell me to walk and I'll run

Tell me to jump and I'll fall

There's no pretending I can withstand
your pull, your silence, your
strangeness, all of it commands.

There must always be a consequence

That only I will know

When I decide to transition to a new
stance, or go.

Hunger

Return to me

When the purple clouds freckle the sky

And my pillar candles are burning

I see the hands of your watch turning,

Backwards.

I'm starving.

Steadily awaiting your words

The curling of your toes

When you finally verbalise,

Passwords.

And then stay,

You don't want to anyway

But you'll save your own fingers,

Fractures.

I turn to you,

My heart speckled black

A ladybird's back

Wings tucked tightly,

Away.

The heart whisperer

Who has learnt the skill to

Quiet the mind

And in so,

Heighten the heart's voice?

The music which shoots through veins,

Weaves a tapestry of euphoric

drowsiness.

Who can quieten her noise?

Like an apprentice's needle

Fifth times the charm.

Finding meaning in words which do not

exist.

Who has learnt the ways of managing

the ebb and flow

Of the heart's reluctant slow

Of love's hyperbolic tableau?

O heart, the grandest instrument of love,

play on,

Give me excess of it.

This

My saviour and sanctum.

A transcript: the words from voiceless

conversations.

A release of all my worldly frustrations.

Plath and Kaur and all the great women

of before

Knew the power of poetry.

The freedom, the symmetry

The everlasting, the momentary.

I breathe poetry

Like a fish breathes in the sea

Or as carbon feeds the wood of a tree.

It is honest and unforgiving,

And all the fearlessness within me.

Healing

Today I am being honest with myself.
I am creeping through the cavities in
these walls that I so passionately built
To expose myself to the elements I have
so keenly ignored.

There is no use for power if you are not
free.
There is such a desire to be in control,
Such a need for perfection
In a life lacking direction.

For this, there is healing.
Curled next to a wood burning stove
With bunched, dried lavender
And cream melting into my cocoa
I draw, I paint, I write, I sing.

I heal.

And out here, with the icy wind in my

hair,

The solid ground beneath my feet

And oak leaves between my fingers.

I heal.

You ask what you can do for me.

To give to me the gift of time

Would be a kindness

Yet, to accept my autonomy, my power,

my strength

Is what I crave.

I deserve.

Let me return to nature,

To the warmth,

To home, and then far away from it.

That is where I must begin the healing.

Affirmation

Blood,

Coagulate.

Unearth these wounds and

Mend

This month's frayed ends.

Lavandula

I've always loved the scent of lavender

Between my fingers in the garden

On my pillow when I sleep

In the shower, soft skin-deep.

Lavender sugar in my baking

Lavender bottles, umbrellas, pots

Burning oils in the evening

Parma violets, childhood-seeking.

For him the scent was strong

For them it lingered too long

For her it smelt just like-Me.

But, will you bathe in it this time

And take all that they left behind

Breathing deep to savour your find

And treasuring all that is yours-that is
mine?

Daybreak

46

Cold and clean

Dewey blades

Warm sun streaks

Blank page

Towards the fresh

Forwards anew

For we have slept

And time has grew.

True

Sing to me this time

Only words true and fearless

Then I will return.

Opal

I see the world in you

    Swirling green into blue

And the light seems to move

    Pleione, like your daughters

But there's a fragility

    A promise of humility

Let me revel in it.

    At least,

Until they pick at you like they did to
their mother.

Sister

Divine

Fierce

Unstoppable.

How could I want to be anything but
this?

We are

The blood which feeds the earth.

The water flooding high ground.

The resounding sounds

Of choice.

Hear the hoarseness of my voice

See my calloused hands

Gifts passed down from ancestors

Who come to tell me:

'Love your sister'

For no one fights harder than a woman.

You are

Girl you are

The fire at the centre of the earth.

Life swells in you.

An eternal sulphuric pýra

Like great Carda, you breathe life.

Lady you are

The soft Jihvā singing

A pooling stream flowing

Your wisdom,

Like honoured, Saraswati.

Woman you are

The womb of our world

Spiralled buds unfurled

A blooming Freyja, behold!

You do not need to choose

To follow rules

To lay down your dreams

To explain yourself

Seize what is yours

Cease for no one

Savour the honey

And never, ever

apologise for it.

Ashes

I

wake to sage clouds.

The branches of my heart dried out.

Time has stood sentinel

Yet, the earth could not cover you.
Instead you took to air and sea

And though your mumbling cries were
no more, I could still hear them echo
inside of me.

It is us who long to be free.

This whole time

I made excuses

Profusely telling

My own heart to quiet

And, in time, I learnt to be silent

The stillness of calm before the storm.

Who knew it would be you that broke
first?

Not me.

Not the fractured pottery I stuck together
with gold

But the immovable rock which now
wishes to climb the mountain.

Shall we see what's on the other side of
this horizon

Together, or alone?

We know we lost the grip long ago

And your fingertips are sore.

But I'll place my feet in the same places
as before

Almost as if I believe the silence to be
true

I have given it all to you

And I'll keep honouring my promises

Let me keep holding on to you

And these excuses

Which turn my frozen tongue blue.

Lifted

The trees are rustling
differently

A sensual sugar-like sound

And the blackbird sings vehemently

After plucking his meals from the ground

The sky is blue and tender

Soon the sunset will paint brick walls

Then man will strive to render

Old relations over distant calls.

She stops, she smells, she listens

And, all the while, she cries

Very soon we will have forgotten

To give space to nature sublime.

57

Last words

Ink cartridges left askew

The pavement speckled red and blue

Grey clouds collect in patterned pain

Sending forth slight specks of rain

The message spilt was loud and clear

Relevant for all to hear

But upon the find the reader turned

And in the air the silence burned.

By such neglect, time casts its spell

Something only the heart will tell

When words are passed without a care

You ignore the magic of a chance so
rare.

Synthesise

I think I have dropped pieces of me

On this long road

A kaleidoscope of glass and stone

Lost in the haze

Of candy floss mist

The smell of mint still on my breath

I remember

Dipping my fingers

In every dish, for feeling

Touching it to my lips, for healing

Is this where I was meant to be?

In this open land,

impossible to see beyond the hills.

Grass sticks between my toes

Sharp realities under my nose

And how my vision blurs

Why is there a hole-

The edges splintering-

When I have reached the end zone?

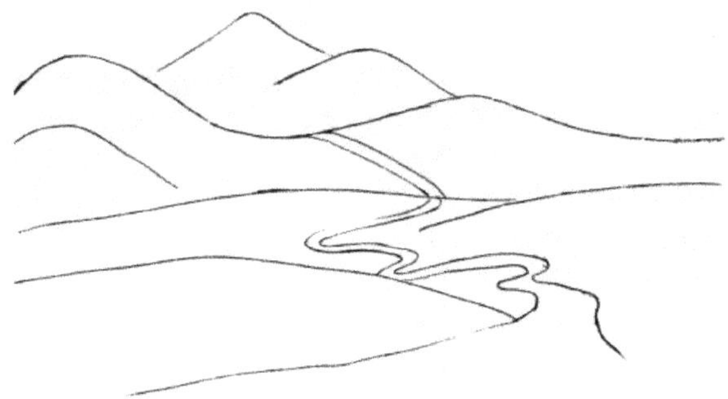

Petal

I guess my thoughts are delicate

Unlike my words.

Torn petals in children's hands;

Silken fragility.

Who would want to toughen them?

Those smooth, yet ragged things.

No. I'll make perfume from their skin

And whisper poetry in

The air.